A Russian Impressionist

Paintings and Drawings by Leonid Pasternak, 1890–1945

L. Pasternak

Paintings and Drawings by Leonid Pasternak, 1890–1945

A Russian Impressionist

SMITHSONIAN INSTITUTION TRAVELING EXHIBITION SERVICE

Washington, D.C.

1987

Published on the occasion of an exhibition organized by the Smithsonian Institution Traveling Exhibition Service and the Pasternak Trust, and circulated between 1987 and 1990. The tour includes the following:

Meridian House International, Washington, D.C.
The Jewish Museum, New York
Lowe Art Museum, University of Miami, Coral Gables, Florida
The Society of the Four Arts, Palm Beach, Florida
The Dixon Gallery, Memphis, Tennessee
Krasl Art Center, St. Joseph, Michigan
Triton Museum of Art, Santa Clara, California
Federal Reserve Bank Gallery, Kansas City, Missouri
The Fine Arts Center at Cheekwood, Nashville, Tennessee

LIBRARY OF CONGRESS CATALOGING-IN-PUBLICATION DATA
Pasternak, Leonid Osipovich, 1862-1945.
A Russian impressionist.
Bibliography: p.
1. Pasternak, Leonid Osipovich, 1862-1945—Exhibitions. 2. Impressionism (Art)—Russian S.F.S.R.—Exhibitions. I. Smithsonian Institution. Traveling Exhibition Service. II. Title.
N6999.P375A4 1987 759.7 87-32091
ISBN 0-86528-038-X

Manufactured in the United States of America

COVER: *Rosalia Pasternak with Little Boris,* 1892, cat. 3

FRONTISPIECE: *Winter View, Moscow,* 1917, cat. 50

Contents

Josephine and Lydia in the Nursery, 1908, cat. 14

Preface

The art of Leonid Osipovich Pasternak (1862-1945), today found in major public and private collections the world over, assures him a place of prominence in the pantheon of nineteenth and twentieth century art. Since Pasternak's death, over a dozen exhibitions, worldwide, have circulated his works, but this is the first to share them with American audiences. And thanks to fortunate circumstances, this exhibition brings to light many paintings and drawings hitherto unavailable for public view. Drawn entirely from family collections, these works reveal an intimate portrait of the man, his family, and his contemporaries, which included Europe's foremost artists and thinkers of the day—Tolstoy, Lenin, Einstein, Rachmaninov, to name a few.

A leading portrait painter, genre scene artist, illustrator, and academician, Leonid Pasternak figured largely in the art worlds of pre-revolutionary Russia and later of the international city of Berlin before the Second World War. Much of his early to mid-career work has remained in Russia, notably in the Tretiakov Gallery, the Tolstoy and Gorky Museums, the Lenin State Library, the State Russian Museum, and the Tolstoy collections, as well as in the art museums of Smolensk, the artist's native Odessa, and other cities. Among the European institutions that own works by Pasternak are the Berlin Kupferstichkabinett, the Neue Pinakothek in Munich, the Musée d'Orsay in Paris, the British Museum, the Tate Gallery and the Victoria and Albert Museum in London, the Ashmolean Museum in Oxford University, and the city art galleries of Bristol, Birmingham, and Southampton. In the United States, Pasternak is represented in the collections of Harvard University, and in Israel, at the University of Jerusalem and the Tel Aviv Museum.

A large body of Pasternak's work has remained in England, in the hands of his family, and it is from the Pasternak Trust, based in Oxford, that this exhibition was drawn. The Trust's collection spans the artist's career; our only limitation, because this is a traveling exhibition, was the necessary exclusion of the splendid pastel drawings, a medium in which Pasternak excelled, as did many of the French Impressionist artists he admired.

Pasternak's commissioned portraits, for which he justly became famous, have invariably been key in past exhibitions. His portraiture again features in the present show, but by and large these works were done whenever inspiration took hold—we see lovingly depicted interiors with his family, perceptive renderings of his friends, charming urban views and landscapes in the impressionistic style. By them, he emerges as a master of the domestic scene and the genre portrait, a pioneer among his contemporaries in the exploration of new subjects, approaches, and techniques in drawing and painting, and historically, a Russian Impressionist.

It is deeply gratifying to be the organizer of this premier Leonid Pasternak exhibition in the United States. The project owes its realization to a great number of people, and I take pleasure in acknowledging them.

It has been a privilege to get to know Leonid Pasternak's English relatives, who are devoted keepers of his legacy. The artist's daughters, Josephine Pasternak and Lydia Pasternak Slater, who appear in so many of the pictures, are invaluable witnesses of the period. Their children are accomplished writers, doctors, and scholars, of varying temperaments and interests, each one actively committed to preserving the family history. To that end, the Pasternak Trust was formed. Trustees Michael Slater, Lydia Pasternak Slater, Ann Pasternak Slater, Nicolas Slater, and Catherine Oppenheimer collaborated with SITES to bring about *A Russian Impressionist: Paintings and Drawings by Leonid Pasternak, 1890-1945*. Together, the heirs of Leonid Pasternak offer an archive of personal memories, feelings, and opinions, and each one has had an impact on this exhibition. Above all, I wish to thank Michael Slater, who has been a valued colleague in shepherding this project from its earliest phase, over unexpected and stubborn obstacles, rescuing it from near collapse, and bringing it to completion, always seeing to the finest detail. Michael's research has also contributed significantly to the catalogue notes. Ann Pasternak Slater is gratefully acknowledged for coordinating the photography, mounting, and conservation of the works in Oxford.

The Pasternak Trust joins me in thanking Judith Chantry of the Ashmolean Museum, Oxford, for her conservation advice and for a splendid job in matting the works on paper. We wish to thank Jane Cunningham, Librarian of the Photographic Survey of the Courtauld Institute of Art, University of London, for providing black and white photographs of the works of art. We are also indebted to Professor Rima Salys of the State University of New York at Binghamton, who generously shared her current research for a catalogue raisonné on Leonid Pasternak with Michael Slater and helped to verify titles, dates, and other matters concerning the works of art. In Oxford I enjoyed the hospitality and advice of Helen and Bill Ramsay, Josephine Pasternak, and my friend Rory Collins, to whom I am most grateful.

The catalyst for the project was James D. Griffin, who first proposed the idea for the exhibition and introduced me to members of the Pasternak family. Jim and his wife Jane followed the project's development and offered welcomed advice and support.

British Airways, longtime friend of the Smithsonian, has generously provided transatlantic transportation for the exhibition. This essential, in-kind contribution greatly offset other expenses of the project. We extend our deep appreciation to British Airways.

Alison Hilton, professor of art history at Georgetown University and specialist in turn-of-the-century Russian art, has contributed a most enlightening introductory essay on the life, milieu, and art of Leonid Pasternak. SITES is honored by her participation and the project much enhanced.

There is a group of people at the Smithsonian whose enthusiastic efforts and good will contributed to the successful realization of this project. I must first thank Peggy Loar, former SITES director, and her acting successor, Eileen Rose, as well as Linda Bell, assistant director for administration, for their heartfelt and attentive support. Acknowledgments are also due Sharon White Senghor of the Smithsonian's Office of General Counsel for her thoughtful advice and counsel.

The production of this exhibition owes a special debt to the Smithsonian's Office of Exhibits Central, under the talented direction of Walter Sorrell and Karen Fort. Diana Cohen, with characteristic enthusiasm and thoroughness, edited the exhibition script; Tina Lynch, with equal skill, designed the exhibition; James Speight's team of artisans produced the handsome frames and silkscreened panels and labels; Kenneth Clevinger and his crew of cabinetmakers were responsible for crating the paintings and drawings. I also wish to thank Joe Goulait, chief of the Smithsonian's color lab, for his superb photography.

Much needed assistance was provided by SITES' able registrars, especially Carol Harsh, who assisted in setting up the exhibition's tour. Frederica Adelman contributed to the educational programs, and Dee Bennett and Liz Hill, with characteristic proficiency, coordinated the publicity of the exhibition.

SITES' editor, David Andrews, was supportive and wise in his approach to the catalogue manuscripts; Alison Hilton joins me in thanking him. As always, Andrea Stevens, SITES' publications director, has gracefully managed the production of the catalogue, and we thank Gerard Valerio for conceiving its handsome design. The good cheer and diligence of exhibition assistant Teresa Murray were vital in bringing this project to fruition.

Finally, we thank the host museums for joining SITES in presenting *A Russian Impressionist: Paintings and Drawings by Leonid Pasternak, 1890-1945.*

ELIZABETH A. DRISCOLL

PROJECT DIRECTOR, SITES

Chronology

1862 Born April 4, in Odessa, to Jewish parents. Young Pasternak develops an early interest in drawing, despite his parents' disapproval.

1879 Begins lessons at the Odessa School of Drawing.

1881 Enters the medical school of Moscow University, in the hope of also studying at the Moscow School of Painting, Sculpture and Architecture.

1882 Still unable to study at the Moscow School of Painting, studies privately with the academic painter, Professor E. Sorokin.

1883 Abandons medicine for law and transfers to the University at Odessa, which permits him to travel abroad. Attends Munich Academy of Art.

1885 Completes law degree and one year military service in Odessa. Meets Rosalia Kaufmann, the pianist.

1888 Moves to Moscow. Paints large-scale genre painting, *A Letter from Home*, purchased by Pavel Tretiakov for his gallery. It is exhibited at the Wanderers' exhibition and favorably reviewed.

1889 Marries Rosalia Kaufmann; they move to Moscow. Becomes acquainted with younger painters Valentin Serov and Konstantin Korovin and others in the circle of Vasilii Polenov, landscape painter and member of the Wanderers; also meets Ilia Repin, leading realist painter. Works on the new review, *The Artist*, and later becomes its art director. Establishes his own drawing school, based on methods of teaching drawing from life used in Munich and Paris.
Visits Paris, where he sees work of French Impressionists.

1890 Son Boris is born.

1892 *The North* magazine commissions him to illustrate Tolstoy's *War and Peace*.

1893 Meets Tolstoy. Second son, Alexander, is born.

1894 Joins the faculty of the Moscow School of Painting, Sculpture and Architecture.

1898 Tolstoy invites him to illustrate *Resurrection*. Exhibits with "World of Art" group in St. Petersburg.

1900 Visits Paris, where his canvas, *Students Before the Examination*, is acquired by the Musée du Luxembourg; this painting and his drawings for *Resurrection* are exhibited at Paris Universal Exhibition.
In Moscow, daughter Josephine is born. Helps to found group called the "Thirty-Six Artists," forerunner of the Union of Russian Artists.

1902 Second daughter, Lydia, is born.

1903 Exhibits at first Union of Russian Artists show, in Moscow.

1904 Invited to be an organizer of the art section of international exhibition of art and industry in Dusseldorf.
Visits Venice.

1905 Elected a member of the Academy of Fine Arts. Abortive revolution of 1905 closes the Moscow School; with his family spends several months in Berlin, where he gets to know Lovis Corinth, Max Liebermann, and other German Impressionists.

1907 From Moscow, travels in Holland, Belgium, and England.

1910 Tolstoy dies. The writer's wife Sonya summons Pasternak to make a final, deathbed drawing of him.

1912 Visits Germany and Italy.

1914 Lithograph, *The Wounded Soldier*, is a great popular success.

1921 Moves to Berlin, where he lives until 1938.

1924 Travels in Egypt and Palestine.

1927 First solo exhibition, at Galerie Hartberg, Berlin.

1932 Second solo exhibition at Galerie Hartberg, accompanied by a monograph on Pasternak with text by critic Max Osborn.

1938 Visits London and prepares for return to Moscow.

1939 Death of Rosalia Pasternak. Moves to Oxford in declining health.

1945 Dies in Oxford on May 31, aged 83.

SELECTED POSTHUMOUS EXHIBITIONS

1958 Memorial Exhibition, Ashmolean Museum, Oxford

1958 *The Russian Scene*, Puskhin House, London

1961 *Russian Art and Life*, Hove Museum, England (group exhibition)

1962 Centenary Exhibition, City Gallery, Lenbachhaus, Munich

1962 Centenary Exhibition, City Art Gallery & Museum, Bristol

1962 Centenary Exhibition, Herbert Art Gallery & Museum, Coventry

1969 Exhibition from Private Collections, Moscow

1969 Oxford University Press, Ely House, London

1969 Westfield College, London

1974 Von Maltzahn Gallery, London

1975 Von Maltzahn, representing the London gallery at the International Art Fairs at Basel and Düsseldorf

1978 Scottish Arts Council Touring Exhibition shown at:
Crawford Centre for the Arts, University of St. Andrews
Graves Art Gallery, Sheffield
MacRobert Art Gallery, Stirling
Talbot Rice Art Centre, Edinburgh

1979 Retrospective, State Tretiakov Gallery, Moscow

1980 *Paris-Moscou* (Tolstoy section), Musée Nationale d'Art Moderne, Centre National d'Art et de Culture Georges Pompidou, Paris (group exhibition)

1982 *Moskva-Parizh*, Pushkin Museum of Fine Arts, Moscow (group exhibition)

1982-83 *Leonid Pasternak: 1862-1945*, Museum of Modern Art, Oxford

1987-90 U.S. tour organized by the Smithsonian Institution Traveling Exhibition Service

Self Portrait in a Yellow Robe, 1930s. From the collection of Charles Pasternak and Helen Ramsay.
Photo courtesy of the Pasternak Trust

Drawing from Life
Leonid Pasternak and Russian Art

BY ALISON HILTON

One of the most cosmopolitan and widely respected artists of his generation, Leonid Pasternak spent his childhood in provincial Odessa, studied in Moscow and Munich, taught at the prestigious Moscow School of Painting, Sculpture and Architecture, traveled throughout Europe, lived for several years in Berlin, and, at end of his life, settled in England. Best known as a portraitist and a graphic artist, he left memorable images of his contemporaries—Tolstoy, Gorky, Scriabin, Chaliapin, Rachmaninov, Verhaeren, Corinth, Rilke, and Einstein among others—as well as what are considered definitive illustrations for some of Tolstoy's major works. Beyond this, he was a master of verbal description: his letters and memoirs, found years after his death by his daughter Josephine, present an engaging picture of the man, his family and friends, his experiences and opinions of the art world, and his outlook on life.[1]

Pasternak's art is easy to appreciate—it is direct, unpretentious, and predominately of familiar subjects. A firm believer in constant sketching and life drawing, Pasternak worked in all media (charcoal, pencil, watercolor, and pastel as well as oil). He is also credited with some technical innovations in lithography, but he was not interested in experimentation for its own sake. He vehemently rejected the "violent influence" of Cubism and Futurism and other "temporary epidemics" associated with the avant-garde at the beginning of the twentieth century. He deplored both the outdated and restrictive insistence on Russian subject matter by the leading realists of the preceding generation as well as the European bias and (to his mind) snobbish aestheticism of the vocal younger artists who came to the fore at the turn of the century. As a teacher, he tried to help his pupils become "interesting artists, original and unlike one another."[2] As an artist, he aimed for firmness and precision of drawing and freshness of execution. Above all, he valued truth to the nature of the subject and honesty in his own responses.

It comes as a surprise to realize how easy it is to nod in recognition at Pasternak's paintings and drawings; the viewer is normally only aware of a sense of naturalness and, especially in interior group scenes, a warm unifying light or a visual harmony created by echoing contours. The artist's son, Boris Pasternak, once wrote, "Art is full of things that everyone knows about."[3] He was thinking of music and literature as well as the visual arts, but the comment is especially true of his father's work.

THE FORMATION OF AN ARTIST

Throughout his long life, encompassing an era of rapid change in the art world as well as revolution in the social and political spheres, Pasternak was a liberal, but not a political activist, and current issues only rarely found expression in his art. Nevertheless, in order to understand Pasternak's position and the relationship of his art to that of his contemporaries both in Russia and abroad, it is important to place his biography[4] within the framework of the major events that affected Russian art in the latter part of the nineteenth century, especially the rise of Realism in the 1860s and '70s and the emergence of independent artists' groups.

Pasternak was born in 1862, began drawing lessons in 1879, studied in Munich between 1883 and 1886, and made his debut as an exhibiting artist in 1889. By the mid 1890s, he had a solid reputation as a painter and illustrator, and was on the faculty of the Moscow School; around 1900 he was active in forming two new exhibiting associations, including the important Union of Russian Artists. During the next several years he traveled and exhibited in Europe; after the revolution, the Pasternaks moved to Berlin and lived there until the rise of Nazism and threats of war sent them to England in 1938. Pasternak died in Oxford in 1945.

The Realist Movement

The key event in the Russian art world of the nineteenth century was really a gesture of independence, in 1863, on the part of some senior students at the Imperial Academy of Arts in St. Petersburg. In a spirit of reform, the officials had made changes in the final competition requirements, allowing students to choose their own subjects. But the officials went back on their agreement, so Ivan Kramskoi and his comrades refused to paint the set theme—Odin in Walhalla, from Germanic mythology—and resigned from the Academy, thus forfeiting all chances of official rank and success. They formed a cooperative workshop, or *artel,* to provide a modicum of economic security as well as moral support. Partly inspired by the writings of Nikolai Chernyshevsky, who declared that art should reflect reality and serve to explain the issues of real life, many of these artists, and others attracted to their views, chose to paint genre scenes and portraits, or scenes from Russian history, in preference to biblical and mythological themes.

There was no sharp dividing line separating their works from those of the Academicians either in subject or style, but there was, gradually, an increasing acceptance of "scenes from life," as genre paintings were called. By the end of the decade, a group of artists from Moscow joined the artel members in forming a new organization, the Association for Traveling Art Exhibitions, whose purpose was to hold exhibitions not only in St. Petersburg and Moscow but in several of the larger provincial cities, thus "awakening a love of art in the people" and improving the market for art work.[5]

Besides such artist members as Kramskoi and Nikolai Ge, Vasilii Perov, Grigorii Miasoedov, Vladimir Makovsky, and the younger Ilia Repin and Vasilii Polenov, who joined later, the two most important figures in the formation of the new movement were Vladimir Stasov, the influential music and art critic who advocated a national Russian school of art, and the collector Pavel Tretiakov, who in his twenties conceived the idea of building a unique national collection of the best of Russian art (the Tretiakov Gallery in Moscow is his legacy).

The history of the Association (known as the *Peredvizhniki,* translated "Wanderers" or "Itinerants") is complex, full of competing personalities and apparent ideological contradictions. Here it is sufficient to note that after a shaky beginning, the group became extremely successful, and eventually the differences between the Peredvizhniki and the Academy faded (indeed the St. Petersburg exhibitions were held in the Academy halls and in the 1890s several members joined the Academy teaching staff). Paintings of humble subjects, even of the poor and downtrodden, were purchased by wealthy merchants, nobles, and members of the imperial family—Ilia Repin's famous *Barge Haulers on the Volga* was bought by the Grand Duke Vladimir for his billiard room.

When Tsar Alexander III succeeded to the throne in 1881, the Peredvizhniki came into their own, since the Tsar believed that art could convey the idea of official nationalism that he identified with his reign. He founded a museum of Russian art in St. Petersburg, and frequently outbid Tretiakov in his eagerness to acquire paintings showing his notion of Russian life. Of course, many of the Peredvizhniki benefited, and some virtually painted to order; but, by the mid 1880s, both the critical edge and the sense of purpose manifest in the beginning had dulled. However, their work still showed an undeniable emphasis on human experience (as opposed to myth), a general tendency to work from life and to avoid academic idealization, and a strong feeling for the Russian landscape.

Early Life and Education

Pasternak's formation as an artist took place far from the centers of activity and controversy, but in retrospect his early interests and artistic choices bear the marks of his time. In his autobiographical notes, Pasternak fondly recalled the assortment of characters—Ukrainian peasants, Tartar pedlars, mysterious gypsies, and petty landowners "straight out of Gogol,"[6] who would put up at the small inn near the market managed by his own Jewish mother and father—and the scenes of festivity and daily work that stimulated his skills of observation and imagination. He was sent to school by self-sacrificing parents, who hoped he would become a doctor or lawyer and did everything they could to discourage his love of drawing, even to the point of burning his sketches. At school he continued to draw, and enjoyed great success with caricatures of his friends and teachers; he also had drawings published in local journals, and in 1879—his senior year—he was given the chance to take lessons, free of charge, at the Odessa School of Drawing. Although the school was small, several other artists, notably Mikhail Vrubel, were trained there.

Leonid Osipovich Pasternak as a schoolboy in Odessa, ca. 1870. *Courtesy of the Pasternak Trust*

Out of a sense of obligation to his parents, Pasternak decided to enter the medical school of Moscow University in 1881, in the hope of studying simultaneously at the famous Moscow School of Painting, Sculpture and Architecture. But he arrived too late to enter that year: the one place left was given to another candidate, a young woman artist whom he later came to know well, Countess Tatyana Tolstaia. Instead, he entered the private studio of the academic painter Sorokin, where he learned something about technique but realized that the conventional approach to rendering figures, without looking at a model, would be of no use to him. At the same time, he developed a distaste for dissection, and decided to switch from medicine to law, and transfer to the university at Odessa, where the liberal regulations allowed students to travel abroad to attend the lectures of foreign professors, and to remain as long as they wished provided they took the required exams each year. The decision to go to Munich to study was, Pasternak felt, the real beginning of his systematic artistic education.

Pasternak loved Munich, with its informal atmosphere and intense artistic life. With only meager funds, he seems to have lived on bread and horseradish, but he was hungry for art and contact with other artists. He felt inspired by his classes at the Academy, especially life-drawing with Ludwig Herterich, and he was consistently at the top of his class. His greatest pleasure was visiting the art museums—the Alte Pinakothek, and the Neue Pinakothek, which housed the Kupferstichkabinett and kindled his first interest in engraving and etching. Although he learned a great deal from Herterich, after he moved on to the painting class later that year (1883) he became disillusioned with the techniques taught there, and had no interest in the highly praised but "boring" historical paintings of the Munich professors. For painting, he believed, he had to go to Paris, but first he had to return to Odessa, pass the law examinations, and graduate from the university; then he had to do his military service.

While completing his various obligations and getting ready for the "decisive change" in his life, Pasternak became acquainted with Rosalia Kaufmann, a brilliant young pianist who had been performing since the age of eight, and who then was supervisor and teacher in the master class for exceptional students at the Odessa Music School, a branch of the St. Petersburg Conservatory. Pasternak soon realized that he was deeply in love, but he hesitated, "being uncertain of myself and unwilling to stand in the way of Rosa's career" and afraid that the single-minded dedication required for art prohibited family life.[7] After nearly a year of worry, which brought on a serious illness, Pasternak decided to put off the trip to Paris and instead go to Moscow, where he would work on a large painting that would sum up what he had learned up to that point and also reflect his own experiences. The painting was to be a large picture of garrison life. Rosalia Kaufmann meanwhile stayed at work in Odessa; they planned to get married early in 1889.

Moscow and A Letter from Home

At this point, Pasternak felt his conflicts resolved; he experienced personal happiness and professional success. He worked well in Moscow. The large canvas, entitled *A Letter from Home,* shows three young soldiers in a barracks room, one lying on a cot smoking, one perched on the edge of the cot, leaning forward, hands holding an opened envelope. Unable to read, he has given his letter, perhaps his first news from home, to a comrade, and he listens intently, eyes unfocussed, while the third soldier reads painstakingly, holding the letter up to catch the light from the window behind him. There is a hint of a view through the window; there are pictures on the walls, mainly cheap popular prints, a photograph of the imperial family, and an icon in the corner. Besides setting the scene, this background—light filled and varied in color and texture—sets off the bulk of the three figures.

For all its apparent simplicity, the painting produced a strong impression on all who saw it, and people began to talk about it long before it was finished.[8] Pavel Tretiakov, the great collector of Russian art, came to see it, and purchased it on the spot, ensuring it a place in his gallery. Pasternak was overjoyed, counting Tretiakov's visit one of the most important events in his life and a good omen for his professional debut. The painting was accepted for the exhibition of the Peredvizhniki, noticed by artists, and mentioned favorably in reviews, and this gave Pasternak a great deal of optimism for the future.

Even more important than the immediate success of the picture was the opportunity for Pasternak to get acquainted with the most forward-looking group of artists in Moscow, centering around Vasilii Polenov, some twenty years older, a professor of landscape painting at the Moscow School and a member of the Wanderers. Through Polenov, he also met Ilia Repin, by then recognized as the leading

Leonid painting *en plein air* in his Odessa garden with Rosalia and their son, Boris, ca. 1895.
Courtesy of the Pasternak Trust

A Letter from Home, 1889. From the collection of Charles Pasternak and Helen Ramsay.
Photo courtesy of the Pasternak Trust

The Pasternaks' flat lies in the background, between the Cathedral of Christ the Savior on the left and the Church of the Blessed Virgin and the Golovteyev mansion to the right. *Courtesy of the Pasternak Trust*

realist painter of historical and contemporary scenes as well as portraits. Both artists became and remained good friends with Pasternak. Both were also genuinely interested in the younger artists, believing that this generation would bring about a true renewal of art in Russia.

A Shift in Russian Art

At the time of Pasternak's debut at the Wanderers' exhibition, a shift of balance in the art world was beginning to be felt. With their material success, inevitably some of the Peredvizhniki grew conservative both artistically and philosophically. Some of the senior members of the association were reluctant to allow younger artists to exhibit in the annual shows or be admitted to membership. In fact the original charter, which allowed artists to become members once their works were accepted for exhibition, was reinterpreted in the most rigid way to set up a distinction between full members and mere "exhibitors" with no rights, so that some of the most talented younger artists, like Valentin Serov, had to wait years before being granted membership. Konstantin Korovin exhibited nine times but was never admitted, and Mikhail Vrubel never had a work accepted. "Today, with so many possibilities for exhibiting," Pasternak later wrote, "it may seem strange that we tried so hard to take part in an uncongenial society . . . but the Association of Traveling Exhibitions was the single significant artistic organization, and only by participating in its exhibitions could beginning artists have any chance of acquainting the public with their work."[9]

Only Repin, Polenov, and Ge were supporters of the young artists, and they were always overruled. Polenov was especially gloomy about the "protectivism and nepotism" rampant at the meetings, and blamed the older members for "a general stagnation of mind" and "hatred of all that is young and fresh."[10] In this atmosphere it is no wonder that the young artists of Polenov's circle were nervous about the results of the voting for the yearly exhibitions, or that Pasternak was overwhelmed at his good fortune in being accepted.

Polenov held regular "drawing evenings" at his house, and these meetings were as important to Pasternak as to the other artists who attended—Elena Polenova, Vasilii's sister, Serov, Korovin, Isaak Levitan, Mikhail Nesterov, and Abram Arkhipov, among others. They all took turns posing, and all freely criticized each other. Even more important than the practice in drawing was the habit of mutual interest and support. At one point several of these artists took the step of petitioning the council of the Peredvizhniki for the right to take a more active role in organizing the exhibitions,[11] and it was the same group that became the nucleus of the new exhibiting societies a decade later.

During these early years in Moscow, Pasternak began sending his drawings, mainly genre studies, to various small journals. When a new review, *The Artist,* appeared, Pasternak sent in some studies and was immediately asked to become artistic director. He also began giving private drawing lessons and soon decided to establish his own drawing school based on the methods of teaching drawing from life used in Munich and Paris. The school was successful enough to pay living expenses (both Polenov and Repin sent him pupils), and the progress of his students, combined with his own increasing reputation as an artist, finally led to an invitation to join the staff of the Moscow School of Painting, Sculpture and Architecture.

The Moscow School

At this point, in 1894, Pasternak felt that he was free of financial worries. His wife had given up her concert career, a fact that still made Pasternak feel guilty, though she played regularly. Fortunately, she had as a friend Olga Trubnikova, a former colleague at the Odessa Music School, who had married Valentin Serov at about the same time Rosalia married Leonid Pasternak. Rosalia also kept in touch with other musicians, and Pasternak constantly expressed his gratitude to her for opening the world of music for him.

They now had two children: Boris was born in 1890, Alexander in 1893, and their two daughters, Josephine and Lydia, were to be born in 1900 and 1902. Boris Pasternak wrote a vivid picture of growing up in an apartment at the Moscow School (this was one of the staff benefits), especially the exciting days when they watched from the balcony as paintings were uncrated for the opening of the traveling exhibition, and seeing his father, other teachers, and the art students going about their work.[12]

In the elder Pasternak's own estimation, the Moscow School was at the time one of the best teaching institutions anywhere, both in the diversity of its program and in the exceptional quality of its teaching staff—Serov, Levitan, Arkhipov, and other members of the Polenov circle besides himself. His 1902 pastel study of faculty members at a staff meeting gives a sense of the typical convivial atmosphere there. Much in the spirit of Polenov, Pasternak felt that he was working in "collaboration" with his students, and learning while he was teaching.[13]

It was partly their mutual trust and their sympathy for the situation of younger artists trying to find opportunities to exhibit and finally their impatience at the continued obstructionism of the conservative Peredvizhniki that led members of this group to form the core of a new artistic community. The first group, called the "Thirty-Six Artists," established in 1900, and the Union of Russian Artists, founded in 1903, which flourished until 1923, had the aim of abolishing the art bureaucracy and holding juryless exhibitions to allow "complete freedom of creative work and self-determination" for all artists.[14] Pasternak believed that his teaching at the Moscow School and his involvement in the Union were among his most important contributions to Russian art.

TOLSTOY AND *RESURRECTION*

Pasternak's meeting with Leo Tolstoy was one of the turning points of his life, and his long friendship with the author and his family is the subject of a detailed memoir, which he intended to publish separately.[15] In 1892 the editors of the periodical *The North* commissioned Pasternak, along with several other artists, to make color illustrations for *War and Peace*. He plunged into the work eagerly, but after he had finished the sketches and begun to work out details, he kept wishing he could ask how the author himself envisioned them, though he lacked the courage to approach the great man. Finally the opportunity came about by chance.

Pasternak had a work accepted for the Wanderers' exhibition in 1893, a large canvas called *The Debutante*. He went to the vernissage to see how the piece was hung and in the midst of the noise and activity of last-minute arrangements, he noticed a commotion near the entrance and heard the words "Tolstoy is coming." Pasternak recalls how his friend, Konstantin Savitsky, wanted to introduce him, but he hung back timidly. Meanwhile, Tolstoy walked around the exhibition, greeting painters, and looking intently at the pictures; as he drew nearer to Pasternak's work, the young painter nearly choked with excitement and fear. When Tolstoy stopped, Savitsky started to mention Pasternak's name, but Tolstoy interrupted, "Yes, I know him; I have been following his work." Pasternak was overwhelmed with delight and confusion; but it was only by the end of the viewing that he managed to say something about his illustrations, at which Tolstoy invited him to come to tea the next week and bring his drawings.

Tolstoy was so cordial at the next meeting that Pasternak began to feel at ease, and responded to the writer's exclamations of pleasure at the illustrations for *War and Peace*. He also met Tolstoy's daughter Tatiana, the artist who had won the place at the Moscow School that he had tried for years before. Later, Pasternak made many visits to Khamovniki, the Tolstoy house in Moscow, and to the country estate Yasnaya Polyana. Rosalia Pasternak sometimes accompanied him, and played piano for the group.

Because he thought so well of Pasternak's drawings, Tolstoy invited the artist to listen to a reading of a work in progress and later asked him to illustrate *Resurrection,* his novel about prison and exile. Tolstoy was in a hurry to complete the work

Boris and Alexander Pasternak in Sailor Suits, ca. 1903. From the collection of Charles Pasternak and Helen Ramsay. *Photo courtesy of the Courtauld Institute of Art*

because he planned to have it serialized in the Russian periodical *Niva* and in several foreign journals in order to raise money to help a religious sect, the Dukhobors, emigrate to Canada. Pasternak recalls his urgent journey to Yasnaya Polyana, his days spent reading the manuscript, and his evenings talking with Tolstoy. Even while the first parts were being serialized, Tolstoy made changes, some of them apparently in response to Pasternak's sketches. Pasternak worked mainly in Moscow, where he visited gambling dens, the criminal court, and even prisons in order to gather material. He also had to work out convincing portraits of the main characters, and often his depictions turned out to be virtual likenesses of the real characters Tolstoy had in mind when he wrote.

In many ways, Pasternak felt, his work was closer to collaboration than just illustration. The constant, feverish work to complete and dispatch drawings to meet the deadlines and the artist's justifiable pride in his accomplishment were prelude to severe disappointment when he saw the reproductions. Poor technically, they conveyed none of the subtlety or forcefulness of the original watercolors. He could not back out because of the terms of the contract, but eventually the quality of the reproductions, at least in the foreign journals, did improve, and a year later he was able to exhibit the originals in Paris. Pasternak met people from the distant provinces who told him that they almost lived from issue to issue of *Niva,* waiting eagerly for the drawings that for them provided an extraordinary vision of life and suffering. He was gratified when one critic commented that the artist had shown himself "adequate to the author's own artistic understanding," but most of the praise was far more lavish than this.[16] Exhausting as it was, his

Facing page:
Rosalia, Boris, Leonid, and Alexander Pasternak (from left to right) in their flat provided by the School of Art, Architecture and Sculpture in central Moscow, 1905. *Courtesy of the Pasternak Trust*

Josephine and Lydia with their father, Leonid Pasternak, on the dacha steps in the village of Raiki, where the family spent summers outside of Moscow, in 1908. *Courtesy of the Pasternak Trust*

work on the *Resurrection* illustrations was probably Pasternak's most completely satisfying artistic experience.

Over the next several years, Pasternak made numerous portraits of the writer and sketches of the Tolstoy family. One such work, a pastel of the family in their sitting room in artificial evening light, was done in response to a commission from the Musée du Luxembourg, asking Pasternak and four other Russian artists to contribute scenes showing Russian life. Pasternak thought that the Tolstoy family was the most interesting Russian subject he could choose.

When Tolstoy died, his wife Sonya summoned Pasternak to make a final, deathbed drawing of him. Pasternak did not include this in his memoirs, but a few rough lines found in his notebooks suggest that he meant to recall the moving scene. "Must write here about Sonya and the tragedy of Leo Nikolaevich. Death, death-mask, Mikhailo. Trip with Borya to Astapovo."[17]

IMPRESSIONISM AND OLD MASTERS

Pasternak finally had the chance to make the long-delayed trip to Paris in 1889, after his second exhibition with the Wanderers. It was at this time that he got to know the Polenovs and other younger Moscow artists, most of whom shared an interest in the increasingly popular style known as Impressionism. Pasternak has often been called a "Russian Impressionist," and his affinity for impressionistic treatment of figures and environments has been recognized. But the term was used by Russian artists at the time not to designate a specific art movement, but rather to suggest an approach to art, the rendering of certain effects and feelings for a subject.

The Paris Exposition and the 1890s

Serov, Levitan, Nesterov, and Polenova also visited Paris in 1889 to see the Universal Exposition, and their letters about what they saw and admired are revealing.[18] They unanimously singled out Jules Bastien-Lepage as the outstanding artist, and no one even mentioned Manet, Monet, Pissarro, or the other authentic Impressionists represented in the exhibition. Nor did any of the other artists who went to Paris during the next few years—including Korovin, Ivanov, or Polenov—ever single out individual Impressionist artists for special comment. One reason for this was that Sergei Tretiakov, Pavel's brother, owned one of Bastien-Lepage's most striking works, *Village Love;* the artists of Polenov's circle admired the work and looked forward to seeing more like it.[19]

As a large-scale genre painting on a slightly sentimental subject with melancholy overtones, *Village Love* was clearly an inspiration for ambitious genre paintings by the younger artists; Pasternak's *Letter from Home* belongs to this type. Moreover, most of the Russian artists, with the notable exceptions of Levitan and Polenov, were far more interested in people than in landscape, and most of them considered communication of some human feeling more important than such technical effects as "incomplete drawing" and "vanishing" patches of contrasting colors, which most people associated with French Impressionism.[20]

It is obvious, though, in looking at the work done by Pasternak and his friends during the early 1890s, that they did learn a great deal in Paris, especially about the rendition of light and atmosphere and about the possibilities of a quick, sketch-like stroke to suggest movement and immediacy. Pasternak always carried a small, pocket-sized notebook so that he could sketch at any moment and train himself to capture the most fleeting impressions of movement. He had an ideal subject ready at hand in his small children, with their constant, un-self-conscious activity. Even without any physical motion, Pasternak conveys a sense of a precise moment in other domestic scenes of the 1890s, the old nurse sewing by lamplight (cat. 2), the artist's cousin Karl Pasternak pausing for a moment over his books as he listens to Rosalia at the piano (cat. 18). He worked quickly and decisively, even in more finished portraits and genre scenes.[21]

Another characteristic of this period, partly a matter of individual inclination but perhaps encouraged by the example of French Impressionist art, is the abandonment of storytelling in favor of a self-sufficient slice of life. The contrast between two of Pasternak's most successful genre pieces, *Letter from Home,* done just before his trip, and *Students Before the Examination,* done in 1895 and exhibited in Munich and Paris (purchased by the Musée du Luxembourg and now in the Musée d'Orsay), is a case in point. The latter painting also depicts figures in a softly lit room, young men each absorbed in their thoughts, but the composition is slightly more horizontal, the figures placed further back, and the scene lacks the monumentality and tension of the earlier work. Like many of his fellow artists at this time, Pasternak seems to have rejected the belief of the earlier Realists that serious philosophical or emotional content was necessary in a work of art.

Of course by 1895, Parisian avant-garde art had gone far beyond this stage; exhibitions seemed to be dominated by symbolism or, in the opinion of Russian visitors, by bizarre and unhealthy themes, quasi-religious "inner visions" rendered in "horribly bright colors and crude contours," or indecipherable, "foggy" and "unconstructed" forms.[22] Pasternak apparently had no interest in the more eccentric aspects of contemporary French art, but he was quite ready to experiment with new techniques for the sake of flexibility and variety. He used pastels a great deal around this time (although he generally painted in oils when he intended to send a work to an exhibition because of the fragility of the pastel medium and the difficulty of transport). He was also highly attuned to the value of the sketch, and he was among the artists invited to participate in the unprecedented *Exhibition of Sketches and Artistic Experiments,* which Repin organized in 1896.[23]

Foreign art periodicals were of considerable value for Pasternak, the Polenovs, and other friends. Besides *The Studio* and other major publications, Pasternak regularly read the small German paper, *Petersburger Herold,* and was greatly impressed by the quality and impartiality of the art reviews. At the end of the 1890s, he was briefly in contact with the St. Petersburg "World of Art" group; he appreciated the importance of their exhibitions and their journal, *Mir iskusstva,* both of which presented Russian art side-by-side with Western art. But, like some other Russian artists, he found it difficult to reconcile his distrust of the cliquishness and European mannerisms of the group's leaders, notably Benois, with a genuine liking for the energetic and friendly Diaghilev. On the whole, he considered their art inauthentic and feared that their journal conveyed a pretentious and fallacious view of Russian art.[24] Later, when he lived in Germany, Pasternak had the chance to be more directly involved with European publications; he got to know some of the editors and writers, and several of his drawings were published in *The Studio* and *Meister der Farbe.*[25]

Travel Abroad

Pasternak traveled abroad a good deal during the early years of the century, and at last he could do so in some comfort. In 1904, he was invited to be one of the organizers of the art section of the international exhibition of art and industry in Dusseldorf, and afterwards he went to Venice, fulfilling a dream he had had since his student days. He visited Venice again in 1912 and 1924, on these later occasions also visiting Florence, Siena, Perugia, Assisi, and Pisa.

In 1905, Pasternak took his family to Germany for several months; during the abortive 1905 revolution, the Moscow School was occupied by revolutionary student groups. Even though Pasternak was somewhat sympathetic to their cause, there was actually danger for those living in the school's apartments; eventually the buildings were occupied by the Moscow garrison, and the school was closed. While traveling in Italy—and in Germany, the Netherlands, and England—Pasternak regularly visited museums and made small oil copies of his favorite masterpieces. He attached a palette to the bottom of a small box, which also contained paints and brushes, stretched a small canvas on the open lid, and—holding this device—he usually made a quick oil copy in about an hour. These quick copies, his "gallery of old masters," included works of Orcagna and Bennozzo Gozzoli, three Tintorettos, a Veronese, two Rubenses, two Van Dycks, a Velasquez, and two Rembrandts.[26]

Of all artists, Pasternak held Rembrandt in the highest esteem. He had discovered Rembrandt's etchings during his student visits to the Kupferstichkabinett in Munich, and he continued to study Rembrandt's work, especially his etchings and paintings on biblical subjects. He was so moved by Rembrandt's humanism and by his profound understanding of the Old Testament and the Jewish ethos that he even wrote a small book about this idea.[27]

Interested as he was in keeping up with current art, Pasternak, like the majority of his contemporaries, reserved his most sincere admiration for the old masters and his most persistent efforts for the task of achieving the universality and humanism that he found in the great art of the past.

Before and After the Revolution

Pasternak was back in Moscow in 1906, and continued to live and work there through the war years and the 1917 revolution until 1921, although the family made another trip abroad, mainly to obtain treatment for Rosalia Pasternak's heart condition. Both Leonid and his son Boris recall the stimulating, feverish atmosphere of those days: "New publishing houses began popping out of the ground like mushrooms, concerts of new music were given...one after another there opened exhibitions of pictures by...different groups, such as the World of Art, the Golden Fleece, the Jack of Diamonds, the Donkey's Tail, and the Blue Rose....The young people joined these movements."[28] Pasternak distrusted these factions and, as the radical, nihilistic attitude seemed to grow among students, he became convinced of "the utter pointlessness of every activity and the complete uselessness of any endeavor to help the School."[29] At one point he tried to resign, but the administration persuaded him to stay.

Pasternak began to introduce students to new techniques of graphic art at this time, and became involved in efforts to introduce new publications with quality illustrations—an interest he continued throughout his career. During the First World War, Pasternak did a poster for the city of Moscow; copies were sold in aid of war victims. The motif was simple, a bandaged soldier leaning against a wall, but the technique was exceptional for the time: the artist drew in colored crayon on the largest lithographic stone available, so that the prints would all, in a sense, be originals. The poster was reproduced throughout Russia, and the English magazine *The Studio* also ran a special edition of the print.

Pasternak's efforts to make superior quality prints available to ordinary people took on a new relevance with the revolution. *The Wounded Soldier* was reprinted by the State Publishing House, and the artist was also asked for some portraits of public figures, scenes of meetings, and other events. Among the records of this time are a watercolor study of the Meeting of Soviets (1918) and a few drawings of Lenin. Although Pasternak maintained a positive attitude toward the new Soviet government (he kept his Soviet passport even after he finally moved to England), it became more and more important to return to Germany for the sake of his wife's health. He finally resigned from the school and, in 1921, when foreign travel again became possible, he and his wife and daughters went to Berlin.

Berlin, Palestine, and England—the Last Years

Professionally, the time Pasternak spent in Berlin in 1906 and again in the 1920s and '30s was highly satisfying. He worked intensively, enjoying much better facilities for graphic art than he had in Moscow;[30] he attended concerts, the theater, and receptions, where he met many people who became the subjects of portraits. He published a good deal of work in German periodicals, and he also exhibited at the Berlin Secession. His reputation, especially as a portraitist, grew with each exhibition. A solo exhibition at the Hartberg Gallery in Berlin in 1927 was extremely successful, both economically and critically, and the same gallery gave him a second show five years later. This show was accompanied by a monograph with a text by critic Max Osborn, some autobiographical fragments by Pasternak, including pieces on Tolstoy, Rilke, and Corinth, and fine reproductions, many in color.[31] Throughout this invigorating period, contact with other creative personalities—artists, musicians, writers, philosophers, and scientists—was of great im-

Village of Feldafing on the Starnbergersee, near Munich, 1932-33, cat. 57

portance for Pasternak. Many of his portraits of such people as the poets Emile Verhaeren and Rainer Maria Rilke, philosopher H. Cohen, theologian and historian Adolf von Harnack, dramatist Gerhart Hauptmann, painters Lovis Corinth and Max Liebermann, and physicist, philosopher, and musician Albert Einstein were not only psychologically perceptive but also stylistically freer and technically more experimental than much of his earlier work.[32]

In 1924, when he was over sixty, Pasternak was invited to accompany an expedition to Palestine, and to make a series of drawings and paintings of the area to be published by the Russian art periodical *Zhar Ptitsa.* He felt overwhelmed by the beauty and magic of the scenery, but "tortured" by the sheer speed of the trip, by train and car. He was forced to sketch quickly, just to "create a visual memory," and the resulting works, among his best landscapes, are extraordinarily vivid. On his travels and throughout his time in Berlin, Pasternak tried to look at things in new ways, and find more effective, more visually economical means of rendering familiar subjects. Even as he grew older, he found Berlin extremely stimulating.

At the end of the 1930s, in the face of the increasing threat of Nazism, the Pasternaks decided to return to Moscow. They postponed this difficult trip in order

The artist Leonid Pasternak, late 1920s. *Courtesy of the Pasternak Trust*

to go to England to stay with their daughter Lydia and try to rest and recover their health, and in 1938 went to London.

Rosalia Pasternak died there the following summer, of a stroke. Pasternak felt that his own life had ended. But he recovered and moved with his daughters to Oxford, where he spent the war years. There were constant visitors, including many war refugees; he got to know some of them and continued to paint portraits. Much of his time was spent, at the urging of his daughters, writing his memoirs. But he was pessimistic about the war and worried about the lack of news from his sons in Russia. His last entry for the year 1943 ends with the quotation, "In times of war, the muses fall silent."[33]

PASTERNAK'S LEGACY

Obituaries, posthumous exhibitions, articles, and monographs published in Europe and Russia testified to the great regard in which Pasternak was held at the time of his death in 1945, both as a human being and as an artist. Many writers mentioned the historical importance of his portraits, which form a veritable gallery of notable figures of the turn of the century. Other writers emphasized the artist's ability to handle more modest subjects, especially intimate, domestic scenes, and to make the most subtle moments and human relationships accessible to the viewer. His work has been compared to that of Bonnard and Vuillard, Renoir and even Degas. Pasternak himself pointed out the "inner artistic affinity" between himself and Serov, noting their shared love of the old masters as well as of contemporary art, their willingness to work hard to develop their powers of observation, and the keenness of their interest in people.

But perhaps Pasternak's art is most distinctive—in a period of rampant individualism and self-conscious innovation—for the fact that it is not deliberately attention-getting. The artist seeks to capture the subject and the moment as truthfully as possible, and his technical discipline is such that he can subordinate problems of handling to the requirements of expression. For instance, his striking portrait of the German painter Lovis Corinth seems very rough, awkward, angular, and full of tension: it shows a man who has just recovered from a debilitating stroke and is still struggling, palette in hand, to overcome its painful effects. People who knew Corinth thought the painting a "miracle" and recognized it as the result of the most meaningful contact between an artist and subject, "heartfelt, reverential love," in the words of one writer.[34]

With very few exceptions, Pasternak's subjects were people he knew and loved—Tolstoy, and above all his own wife and children—as well as scenes he wanted to bring to life, and images that evoked the meaning of a literary work. Professionally committed to his goals as artist and teacher, determined to stand up for his principles, yet patient and able to survive setbacks; psychologically well-balanced and resilient; always observing those around him with sympathy and humor but also, sometimes, inward-looking and meditative, Pasternak was an artist who could refine and strengthen awareness and appreciation of the world. He was not an innovator, but rather a preserver—or perhaps a renovator—of traditional, humanistic values in an era of volatile change.

Notes

1. Pasternak's memoirs were published in Russian in 1975 and more recently in English translation. See Leonid Pasternak, *Zapisi raznykh let* (Moscow: Sovetskii Khudozhnik, 1975) and Leonid Pasternak, *The Memoirs of Leonid Pasternak,* translated by Jennifer Bradshaw, introduction by Josephine Pasternak (London: Quartet Books, 1982).

2. Leonid Pasternak, *Memoirs,* p. 57.

3. Boris Pasternak, *I Remember: Sketch for an Autobiography,* translated by David Magarshak (New York: Meridian, 1960), p. 47.

4. See David Buckman, *Leonid Pasternak: A Russian Impressionist* (London: Maltzahn Gallery Ltd, 1974).

5. For fuller accounts of this background, see E.P. Gomberg-Verzhbinskaya, *Peredvizhniki* (Leningrad: Iskusstvo, 1970) and E.K. Valkenir, *Russian Realist Art. The State and Society: The Peredvizhniki and Their Tradition* (Ann Arbor: Ardis, 1977).

6. Leonid Pasternak, *Memoirs,* p. 18.

7. Leonid Pasternak, *Memoirs,* p. 44.

8. Elena Polenova describes the picture as "a wonderful thing in both idea and execution" and her friends' warm responses to it in a letter to E. Mamontova dated February 4, 1889, in E. Sakharova, ed., *V.D. Polenov—E.D. Polenova. Khroniki sem'i khudozhnikov* (Moscow: Iskusstvo, 1964), pp. 411-12.

9. Leonid Pasternak, *Zapisi raznykh let,* p. 58. See also Alison Hilton, "The Art of Ilia Repin." Unpublished dissertation (New York: Columbia University, 1979, p. 173).

10. Letter from V. Polenov to N. Polenova dated February 13, 1889, in Sakharova, *Polenov—Polenova,* p. 249.

11. The petition, March 1890, was signed by Polenova, Ivanov, Serov, Korovin, Levitan, Arkhipov, Pasternak, and Polenov. It is in the Polenov archives, and reprinted in Sakharova, *Polenov—Polenova,* pp. 450-51.

12. Boris Pasternak, *I Remember,* pp. 21-27.

13. Leonid Pasternak, *Memoirs,* p. 56.

14. Leonid Pasternak, *Memoirs,* p. 9. For a full account of this organization, which had nearly 100 members, see V.P. Lapshin, *Soiuz Russkikh Khudozhnikov* (Leningrad: Khudozhnik RSFSR, 1974). Pasternak was both a founding member and a member of the committee of the union (1910-15) and he exhibited every year until 1917.

15. Leonid Pasternak, "Moi vstrechi s Tolstym," published in *Literaturnaia Rossiia* by E. Babaev, November 1964, and in other forms in the Soviet Union; it is also translated and included in *Memoirs* as Part III, "Meetings with L.N. Tolstoy," pp. 125-77.

16. Leonid Pasternak, *Memoirs,* pp. 157-61.

17. *Memoirs,* p. 177. Tolstoy left home on the morning of November 10, 1910, by third-class train. He caught a chill and died of pneumonia in the stationmaster's house at Astapovo, November 20. In *I Remember* (p. 64), Boris Pasternak, who accompanied his father, wrote of a vivid sketch the artist made of the scene at the station.

18. Letter from Serov to Ostroukhov dated September 16, 1889, in A. A. Guber et al., eds., *Mastera iskusstva ob iskusstve,* Vol. VII (Moscow: Iskusstvo, 1970), p. 206; letters from Polenova to Mamontova and Antipova dated September 23 and October 16, 1889, in Sakharova, *Polenov—Polenova,* pp. 438, 440; letter from Nesterov to his family dated July 22, 1889, in A. Rusakova, ed., *Nesterov. Iz Pisem* (Leningrad, 1968), p. 33.

19. Leonid Pasternak mentions how he and Serov were "captivated" by the work of Bastien-Lepage in the 1880s, in *Memoirs,* p. 93 (where the name is mistranscribed). *Village Love* is now in the Pushkin Museum of Fine Arts in Moscow. Pasternak, in his letters, did mention drawings by Monet, Renoir, and Degas. (I would like to thank Rima Salys and Michael Slater for this information.)

20. Korovin, in contrast, practiced these very effects and gained a reputation as a genuine Impressionist. See N. Moleva, *Konstantin Korovin. Zhizn' i tvorchestvo. Pis'ma, dokumenty, vospominaniia.* (Moscow: Akademia Khudozhestv, 1963), pp. 155, 211-229.

21. Lydia Pasternak's description of her father's working methods is quoted in Buckman, *Leonid Pasternak: A Russian Impressionist,* p. 38.

22. Vasilii Polenov and his sister were also in Paris in 1895; Maria Iakunchikova was there between 1892 and 1894; Korovin, Ivanov, and Repin were also there at various times during this period. The phrases quoted here are from several of Iakunchikova's letters to Polenova: January 11, March 30, and May 28, 1892, and May 15, 1894, in Sakhorava, *Polenov-Polenova,* pp. 478, 483, 484, 500.

23. See V. Lapshin, "Repin i 'Vystavka opytov khudozhestvennogo tvorchestva'," *Iskusstvo,* 1974, no. 10, pp. 62-67.

24. Leonid Pasternak, *Memoirs* (introduction), pp. 2-3 and 95-96. Diaghilev himself thought highly of Pasternak and tried to convince him to exhibit with Mir iskusstva instead of the Thirty-Six. Josephine Pasternak recalls that whenever Diaghilev came to Moscow, he would visit Paster-

nak's studio and look at his works with a view to including some in his next exhibition. He wrote to Serov on October 15, 1902, asking him to talk with the Moscow artists Maliavin, Vinogradov, Pasternak, and others, and to get them "out of the claws of the Thirty-Six," adding "they should be 'ours.'" See V.P. Lapshin, *Soiuz Russkikh Khudozhnikov* (Leningrad: Khudozhnik RSFSR, 1974).

25. See Buckman, *Leonid Pasternak,* p. 52.

26. Leonid Pasternak, *Memoirs,* pp. 66-67.

27. Leonid Pasternak and S. Zal'tsman, *Rembrandt and Judaism* (Berlin, 1923), cited in Buckman, *Leonid Pasternak,* p. 54.

28. Boris Pasternak, *I Remember,* pp. 57-58.

29. Leonid Pasternak, *Memoirs,* p. 57.

30. At that time, as now, it was virtually impossible to have one's own printing press; even established artists, like Ivan Shishkin, would continually face police inspectors, suspicious that the press was used to distribute harmful political leaflets. Cf. Leonid Pasternak, *Memoirs,* p. 102.

31. Max Osborn, *Leonid Pasternak* (Warsaw: Stybel, 1932).

32. Leonid Pasternak, *Memoirs,* p. 71. Pasternak's reminiscences of Rilke, Corinth, and Liebermann are on pp. 108-11 and 118-23.

33. Leonid Pasternak, *Memoirs,* p. 78.

34. Leonid Pasternak, *Memoirs,* p. 121. Pasternak quotes a paragraph by critic F. Stahl in the *Berlin Tageblatt,* December 21, 1927.

Leonid and his son Alexander installing the Union of Russian Artists' spring exhibition in Moscow, 1911.
Courtesy of the Pasternak Trust

CATALOGUE OF THE EXHIBITION

BY ELIZABETH A. DRISCOLL

The period in which Leonid Pasternak lived saw a rapid succession of great movements in European art—Realism, Impressionism, Post-Impressionism, Cubism, Fauvism, Futurism, Expressionism, and Surrealism. In Russia, the realist style of the Wanderers dominated the art scene until the early 1890s, when reactions against its strict principles first gave rise to groups of artists seeking change and then, with the new century and revolution, the avant-garde art movements of Suprematism and Constructivism.

It was between the two opposing camps of the traditional and the radical that Pasternak was active. Although he participated in exhibitions both with the Wanderers (it was through them that he launched his career in Moscow in 1889) and with the avant-garde group the "World of Art" (in St. Petersburg in 1898), he was never formally a part of either faction. More an independent, he practiced and taught the French and German academic methods of life drawing and portraiture.

One may view Pasternak as a transitional figure in Russian art, an accomplished artist, and an influential one, given his many commissions and his teaching position at the Moscow School of Painting, Sculpture and Architecture. Although he was essentially a conservative painter deeply tied to Russian traditions in art, he fervently championed individual style and expression, but for the sake of a transcendent beauty and truth rather than for the worldly social ideals that swept up many of his contemporaries.

Pasternak was passionately interested in the European art of the past. He traveled extensively, and his sophistication and international view made him receptive to the French, German, and English ideas of the time. Around 1900 Pasternak took part in forming the Union of Russian Artists, a deliberately informal group of thirty-six younger painters. He exhibited in Moscow in 1903 with the Union, which included already famous artists like Valentin Serov, Konstantin Korovin, Mikhail Vrubel, Isaak Levitan, and many who would become leaders of the next generation. The Union's exhibitions provided a new freedom of expression for Moscow artists, and they reflected the diversity and quality of the teaching staff of the Moscow School of Painting, Sculpture and Architecture. For Pasternak, his teaching and his involvement with the Union, as Professor Hilton notes in her essay, were his two most important contributions to Russian art.

To call Pasternak a "Russian Impressionist" is to relate his work to the impressionist style pioneered by French artists in the last quarter of the 1800s. By the turn of the century, Russia—like America and all of the European countries—had incorporated the ideas of French Impressionism into their own art traditions, with the result that each nation produced a unique reaction to the movement.

In Pasternak's work, the similarities to French Impressionist art are explicit. His use of impressionist techniques of painting are especially evident in his small-scale and more informal works: loose brush work, experiments with pastel and charcoal drawing, compositional devices such as a view into a space beyond the principal scene depicted, and suggested rather than clearly articulated forms. Philosophically, Pasternak and his fellow Russian painters shared with the French the rejection of historical and mythological themes, in pursuit of immediate experience in their art. All sympathized with the realist approach, which stressed the objective recording of nature and contemporary life—thus the prevalence of "slice of life" subjects in both the Russian and French art of the time.

But many of the French Impressionists, influenced by the rapid scientific advances of the day, preferred subjects that, to their minds, allowed the most objective detachment in their art. Monet, Pissarro, and Seurat, among others of the French school, frequently worked in landscapes, where they could fully explore the abstract effects of light, fragmented colors, and time and spatial relations.

Pasternak, by contrast, was more interested in a subjective reality—the inner life of the individual. Portraiture was his metier, but even in his landscapes he nearly always included figures. Professor Hilton points out that Russian Impressionism implies an approach to art rather than a specific movement. The French techniques were not always suited to formal portaiture, at least for Pasternak, because they tended to make sitters secondary to the formal effect, and to dissolve their individuality into the surrounding space. So he borrowed from the French what was true to his goals, in his portraiture as well as in his figure studies, genre scenes, and occasional still lifes, urban scenes, and landscapes. The same seems to have been the case for other Russian Impressionists, such as Korovin and Serov.

But Pasternak never completely abandoned a psychological approach in favor of formalism, as did the French. In this, he was much more influenced by Russian traditions, German painting, and his sojourns to Munich and Berlin.

German art seems to have been a pivotal influence on Pasternak's use of impressionist techniques, as well as on his concern with evoking mood and capturing moments in time, rather than with telling a story or making a moral in the Russian tradition of critical realism. German Impressionism, as practiced by Max Liebermann and Lovis Corinth, with whom Pasternak had close contact in Berlin, was less formal in approach than French Impressionism; it was more expressionistic and more decisive and severe in depicting figures and forms. In the strictest sense, the French Impressionists eliminated line, while the Russian and German Impressionists continued to emphasize sound draftsmanship, rejecting the dissolution of form. Like the Germans, Pasternak retained the psychologically expressive element in his work, whereas the French Impressionists usually treated the subject in a more impersonal way. Pasternak's palette, rather muted and somber in the works through about 1915, bears comparison with that of his Russian contemporaries and the German Impressionists. His later works are vibrant and warm, perhaps showing the influence of German Expressionism. Only rarely did he use the clear, gay colors of the French Impressionists.

All of the paintings and drawings in this exhibition are from the collection of the Pasternak Trust. The works were selected according to the following four categories: *Early Works, Family Scenes and Portraits, Portraits and Studies of Public Figures and Friends,* and *Still Lifes and Scenes of Russia, Palestine, and Germany.* Pasternak produced them in the period from 1890 to 1940, with one work made in the year the artist died, 1945, thus encompassing Pasternak's career from its beginning in Moscow, through his Berlin period, to the final years in England.

Dimensions of works are given in centimeters; height precedes width. Accession numbers beginning with PT (signifying Pasternak Trust) were assigned when the collection was catalogued by the Courtauld Institute of Art.

Early Works

The eleven works in this section, produced from the early 1890s to the turn of the century, are small-scale, intimate scenes that show Pasternak's versatility: in the oils, with his sensitive brush work in the impressionist style; in the works on paper, with his always sound draftsmanship. Notable here is his characteristic ability to use spatial relationships and the play of light to convey mood. His domestic interiors and landscapes show what he did so well in his work—capture a moment in time. In these early pieces, Pasternak emerges as a subjective realist ably armed with the new techniques of Impressionism.

1.

The Artist's Cousin, Karl Pasternak

ca. 1890; watercolor with whites over pencil on paper
24 x 32; PT 398

The subject appears to be dreaming, lost in thought, distracted from his reading by troublesome thoughts or perhaps by the music that fills the room. The figure in the background, playing the piano, is Leonid's wife Rosalia, née Kaufmann (1867-1939), a gifted musician. This drawing is a good example of Pasternak's sensitive characterization of a person close to him, his ability to evoke the mood of the subject or setting, and his subtle development of a "subplot" by extending the composition into another space, in this case into the room beyond.

2.

Nanny Sewing by Lamplight

1890s; watercolor over pencil on beige paper
31.2 x 23.8; PT 399

This is the family nanny who came to the Pasternaks when Alexander was born; she appears again in *Black Sea with Moon, Nurse, and Baby* (cat. 7). "Niania," as she was called, is still fondly remembered by the artist's daughters, Josephine and Lydia. The painter lovingly rendered her voluptuous form by layering the brown and yellow watercolors, which adds to the warm feeling of her portrait. In his memoirs, Pasternak recalled that conveying interior, artificial light was a challenging but interesting task. In this and in his portrayals of Tolstoy (cats. 29 and 30) he achieved the optimum effect: "I had long been interested in light effects at night and I subsequently returned to the problem of rendering the intimate, almost musical quality which lamplight or candlelight can give to a scene."

3.

Rosalia Pasternak with Little Boris

1892; oil on canvas mounted on board
37.5 x 20.5; PT 432

The foreground shows the artist's wife, Rosalia, sewing and his first-born son, Boris, who is about two years old, wearing a pinafore. In the middle ground is a rug and chest, and in the background there is a view of another room, shown in greater detail than the figures in the principal scene. Viewers of this painting have observed the similarity to interiors by the French painter Edouard Vuillard. As in *The Artist's Cousin, Karl Pasternak* (cat. 1), Pasternak has extended the picture space into the room beyond, where we see such objects as an equestrian statue and a sewing machine. And once again, Pasternak has masterfully orchestrated the composition: the delicate detail lavished on everyday objects in the middle- and background is artfully balanced by the impressionistic rendering of the figures and by the unpainted areas of the canvas.

4.

Rosalia Making Jam

ca. 1890; India ink and wash on prepared board
37.8 x 26.2; PT 89

Pasternak's early style of drawing was characterized by detailed and delicate rendering, as shown here. Pen and ink enabled him to make careful and almost dainty strokes. In mood, this is related to *Nanny Sewing* (cat. 2).

5.

Seated Woman in Black Dress

1891; watercolor and pencil on paper
16.5 x 10.7; PT 640

The subject and technique of this painting suggest that Pasternak may have been studying the work of Edgar Degas. He could have seen examples when he visited the Paris Universal Exhibition in 1889. The subject is rendered with the same precision and daintiness as the previous *Rosalia Making Jam,* although the mood is much more impersonal here, as were Degas' figurative drawings.

6.

Dr. Joseph Kaufmann

1897; oil on canvas
29.5 x 21; PT 369

Joseph Kaufmann ("Uncle Osip") was Rosalia's brother, a country doctor much beloved by his family and his practice. In style, this portrait is related to the genre paintings that had won Pasternak success in the Wanderers' exhibitions of the early 1890s. But unlike the Wanderers' narrative and socially motivated realist paintings, Pasternak is evoking the mood of the sitter, as in *The Artist's Cousin, Karl Pasternak* (cat. 1). The sitter seems remote and pensive, which gives the painting a romantic quality.

7.

Black Sea with Moon, Nurse, and Baby

ca. 1896; oil on canvas mounted on board
14.5 x 20; PT 368

In the 1890s Leonid and Rosalia went each summer to Odessa, where they spent the holidays with their parents. Many of the artist's small seascapes, such as this one and *Two Women Seated by the Black Sea* (cat. 8), as well as his landscapes and informal oil sketches, are from these holiday visits. All of the oils were done in a loose, brushy style, which gives them an intimate quality. The nurse is "Niania," depicted in cat. 2, and the baby is Alexander Pasternak, who was born in 1893.

8.

Two Women Seated by the Black Sea

ca. 1896; oil on canvas mounted on board
25 x 35.4; PT 647

By comparing Pasternak's landscapes with those of French Impressionist painters, it becomes apparent that their interests were quite different. Here, Pasternak has concentrated on the mood of the scene, whereas a French Impressionist might have used sparkling colors to emphasize the play of light on the land and sea. Although Pasternak had adopted the free-style brush strokes of the Impressionists (but not their bright palette), in this painting he used figures to personalize the landscape, and endowed it with a meditative quality and a meaning beyond its formal properties.

9.

The Artist's Mother

1900; oil on canvas
14.5 x 20.2; PT 466

"My father accustomed us to a simple, severe, joyless way of life from our childhood," Pasternak said in his memoirs. "We never had any fun or entertained any guests at home. Any display of affection was slighted in each of us, any show of sentiment was mocked.... My mother was the complete opposite, but she—good nature personified—had submitted to him entirely. There was a lyrical side to her nature and she inclined to the artistic. The main feature of her character was compassion, which is the basis of love towards one's fellow men and of love in general."

10.

Asya and Olya

1903; oil on canvas
31 x 26; PT 370

Asya was Leonid's sister Anna; her daughter Olya (Olga) later became professor of classical literature in Leningrad. She later survived the siege there (in 1941-43); her correspondence with her cousin Boris has been published in the United States. This sketch was made in Maloyaroslavetz, a village not far from Moscow.

11.

Rosalia Ironing

ca. 1897; oil on canvas
14 x 20; PT 52

Like the artist's sketch of his mother, this little genre portrait of his wife ironing was probably made in Odessa. During this period, Pasternak was experimenting with quick oil sketches done in an impressionistic manner, which he would later give up for more flexible media in order to record the many scenes of his home life.

Family Scenes and Portraits

Pasternak's teaching appointment in 1894 at the Moscow School of Painting, Sculpture and Architecture was a turning point for him, because it became the scene of a new generation of painters with new ideas, as he recalls in his memoirs: "The Wanderers' main concern in their work at that time was not form or draughtmanship —but plot, pure and simple; a painting was supposed to 'narrate something.' The young artists, like myself, who were grouped around V.D. Polenov, were instrumental in freeing Russian art from its subjugation to plot—and this was true no matter which techniques we used (charcoal, pencil, pastel, etc.). Our generation strove after, and finally achieved, the freedom to work and exhibit pictures using any techniques, and not just oil, as the Wanderers demanded. I remember that watercolours weren't accepted for Wanderers' exhibitions at all at that time."

Pasternak sketched incessantly, and his wife and four children provided excellent subject matter and led him to experiment with various media, which the French Impressionists had also revived and explored: "Very early I experienced the unwieldiness and inflexibility of oil paints in painting portraits, especially of women and children," he wrote, "and I looked for a more convenient method to quickly work from nature." He began working in pastels, charcoal, watercolor, and tempera and produced some of his most beautiful impressionist works in these media. (Quoted in David Buckman, *Leonid Pasternak: A Russian Impressionist.* London: Maltzahn Gallery Ltd, 1974, p. 28.)

12.

Boris

1901; black and sanguine conte crayon on grey Ingres paper
31.3 x 24; PT 651

Boris Pasternak (1890-1960) was Leonid and Rosalia's eldest child, later to become a distinguished poet and translator, author of *Dr. Zhivago,* and Nobel Prize laureate. In 1901 the Pasternaks moved to a new flat within the College, and it was here that Leonid made so many of the drawings of his children. Some of these have been used to illustrate Boris Pasternak's books, *An Essay in Autobiography* and *Safe Conduct*.

13.

Alexander

1901; black and sanguine conte crayon on grey Ingres paper
31.4 x 23.8; PT 652

Alexander Pasternak (1893-1982), later an architect, was Leonid and Rosalia's second child. At this time they lived in Moscow, but spent the summers in Odessa, where both parents had grown up. Alexander's memoirs, *A Vanished Present,* were published in the United States in 1984.

14.

Josephine and Lydia in the Nursery

1908; black, red, and white chalks on beige paper mounted on paper
44.5 x 31.5; PT 408

Josephine (b. 1900) and Lydia (b. 1902) are the two youngest children of Leonid and Rosalia. The energetic style of this drawing distinguishes it from the earlier, more academic portraits of Boris and Alexander (cats. 12 and 13). On seeing some of Pasternak's nursery sketches, his friend and colleague Valentin Serov remarked, "You have mastered the child." This was a welcomed and valued remark from one of Russia's most accomplished draftsmen and portrait painters. (Quoted in David Buckman, *Leonid Pasternak: A Russian Impressionist.* London: Maltzahn Gallery Ltd, 1974, p. 22.)

15.

Lydia's Teddy Bear

1909; black chalk on paper
10.5 x 18; PT 197

Lydia's teddy bear was a present from the family's doctor (Dr. Levin), who was also a family friend. It was, unusually, called "Bärchen" (German for "little bear"), rather than the almost universal Russian "Misha" or "Mishka." Leonid and Rosalia spoke good German, and the children learned it early in their lives (the family had spent 1906 in Berlin, where the children had a German governess). Pasternak's recordings of childhood were very popular with private collectors. His realism is neither emotional nor completely objective, but each of his domestic scenes and portraits has an intimate quality.

1916

16.

The Artist's Daughters Reading

1916; black and red chalks on paper
25.5 x 38; PT 134

Pasternak's lovingly rendered sketches of his wife and daughters possess a tenderness also found in the pictures of women and children painted by such Impressionists as Auguste Renoir and the American, Mary Cassatt.

17.

Coloring Easter Eggs

1916; black, red, and green chalks on paper
25 x 35; PT 90

The figures, from the left, are Lydia, Josephine, Walter Philip, and Rosalia. Walter Philip was a family friend tutored at one time by Boris Pasternak, an experience later reflected in his novella, *The Last Summer.*

18.

Rosalia at the Piano with Her Daughters

1917; black and sanguine conte crayon on paper
32.7 x 25.5; PT 85

Leonid's wife Rosalia was a professional pianist who in her youth had a wide reputation in Russia. Although she gave up her performing career when she married, she continued to play throughout her life, and music was an essential part of life for the Pasternak family and their friends. It was because of his mother's influence that music was so important to Boris Pasternak as a young man.

20.

Josephine Sewing

1917; black and traces of red chalks on buff paper
36.7 x 26; PT 630

In a letter to his father, Boris Pasternak wrote, "I think that your best subjects were Tolstoy and Josephine. How you drew them! Your drawings of Josephine were such that she grew up according to them, followed them in her life, developed through them more than through anything else." (Quoted in David Buckman, *Leonid Pasternak: A Russian Impressionist. London:* Maltzahn Gallery Ltd, 1974, p. 22.)

19.

Lydia Studying Anatomy

1918; black and red chalk on paper
41.2 x 26.2; PT 411

Although only sixteen years old at the time of this sketch, Lydia Pasternak had already completed high school ("gymnasium") and had entered Moscow University to study medicine. As a result of the war and the revolution, there was a typhoid epidemic in Moscow in 1918, and the new government had ordered all medical students over eighteen to help combat it. Lydia (although under the age limit) wanted to join, but her parents, fearing she would be infected, persuaded her to transfer to the faculty of sciences until the epidemic died down. As events turned out, she never fulfilled her ambition to become a doctor.

21.

Boris Pasternak

1922; charcoal on onionskin paper
33 x 25.5; PT 72

Boris was thirty-three by this time, and a recognized writer. In 1921, his parents and sisters had moved to Germany, and in 1923, Boris and his wife, who lived in the Moscow flat with Boris' younger brother, Alexander, were given permission to visit them in Berlin, when this portrait was made. Alexander recalls Boris' return with stories "about the trips to Marburg, the Harz [Mountains], Weimar, the meetings, the new paintings my father had done, my mother's improved health and renewed playing." (From Ann Pasternak Slater, ed. and trans., *A Vanished Present: The Memoirs of Alexander Pasternak.* London: Harcourt Brace Jovanovich, p. 196.)

22.

Lydia in a Shawl

1930; watercolor on paper
35 x 22; PT 76

The watercolor has been applied in an impressionistic manner, and the form of the figure is flattened in space. Pasternak's palette in the later, Berlin years was considerably brighter than during the period in Russia, before 1921.

23.

Rosalia Peeling Apples

probably 1920s; oil on canvas
53.5 x 42.5; PT 429

This painting is quite impressionistic in the application of the paint and in the use of bright colors.

24.

Lydia Cleaning Fish

1924; watercolor and chalk over pencil on paper
48.5 x 37; PT 628

Professor Hilton has remarked that this vividly colored genre scene from the artist's Berlin period recalls still-life studies of fish by Konstantin Korovin, an established Russian Impressionist.

25.

The Artist's Daughters

1922; oil on canvas
33 x 43.5; PT 409

Pasternak was sixty years old by the time he came to Berlin. He spent most of his still quite successful working life producing formal portraits, but continued depicting family members whenever the opportunity arose. Pasternak himself acknowledged the limits of the oil medium; charcoal and pastel, as seen in earlier family scenes, perhaps allowed fuller expression of his talent for capturing the spontaneous moment.

26.

Josephine and Lydia on the Verandah in Molodi, near Moscow

1922 version of original from 1916; oil on canvas
44.5 x 75; PT 359

In this painting Pasternak has experimented in the style of Gauguin, using vivid yellows and flattened, pattern-like forms. The verandah is part of an eighteenth century mansion where the family spent their summer holidays between 1914 and 1916. The owner spent summers abroad, and rented out blocks of rooms to various people, including the Pasternaks and the composer Scriabin.

27.

Study for a Portrait of the Artist and His Wife

ca. 1935; oil on canvas
33 x 48; PT 381

Painted in a brushy, impressionistic style, this would seem to be a study for the dual, half-figure portrait of Leonid and Rosalia (not in the exhibition). The finished self-portrait shows a dashing artist, palette in hand, in a three-quarter view, a pose he often struck, flanked by his devoted wife.

28.

Self-Portrait

1940; charcoal on paper
35.5 x 20.5; PT 187

Using a mirror, Pasternak made many sketches of himself. This is the last one known to his family. At the age of seventy-eight, a year after his move to Oxford, the artist is melancholy in this self-portrait. Pasternak had been forced to leave Germany by the onset of Nazism there; he had come to England, a foreign country whose language he hardly spoke. The war had started, and he was being accommodated in a house of strangers: his daughter's English parents-in-law. Finally, and most crushingly for him, his wife had died the previous year.

Portraits and Studies of Public Figures and Friends

Pasternak's portraiture from the turn of the century to the Second World War represents a gallery of the great thinkers, writers, musicians, artists, scientists, and politicians of the time: Tolstoy, Rilke, Verhaeren, Rachmaninov, Chaliapin, Hoffmann, Scriabin, Serov, Liebermann, Corinth, Einstein, Weizmann, Lenin, and many other prominent figures of Moscow and Berlin. Stylistically, the portraits range from formal bust portraits in oil, to charcoal and pastel narratives with the sitter engaged in activity, to informal pencil sketches. All of them have individuality and presence. Max Osborn, in a review of Pasternak's Berlin exhibition in 1927, wrote, "There are portraits of staggering virtuosity. Pasternak's people all live, natural and full of movement." (Quoted in David Buckman, *Leonid Pasternak: A Russian Impressionist*. London: Maltzahn Gallery Ltd, 1974, p. 71.)

29.

Tolstoy with Family Seated Round the Table

n.d.; oil on canvas
80.5 x 65; PT 357

In 1892, Pasternak had accepted a commission to submit illustrations for *War and Peace*—but not without considerable anxiety, as he wrote in his reminiscences: "With illustrators it is an understandable and natural yearning to show one's pictures to the author and hear his judgment. Even the great Delacroix used to send his Faust illustrations to Goethe for his opinion; yet I could not bring myself to approach Tolstoy. . . . To address myself to such a giant I lacked the necessary courage in those days." At the Wanderers' exhibition in 1893, Pasternak at last met Tolstoy—a meeting "of great significance to me," he said. There "stood Leo Tolstoy in his grey blouse with a leather strip for a belt . . . the great author of *War and Peace*. And he did not look intimidating at all. A very lovable, simple, yet dignified old man who seemed to be ill at ease. . . . Despite his sixty-five years he appeared lively, robust, and of great strength of mind and body." Tolstoy was exceptionally pleased with Pasternak's drawings and invited him in 1898 to illustrate the novel *Resurrection* and stay with the Tolstoys at their estate, Yasnaya Polyana, where the writing and the illustrating of the novel ultimately took place simultaneously. Pasternak became a family friend of the Tolstoys and took many opportunitities to draw and paint the author. (Quoted in David Buckman, *Leonid Pasternak: A Russian Impressionist*. London: Maltzahn Gallery Ltd, 1974, pp. 24-27.)

30.

Tolstoy Reading by Oil Lamp

late 1890s; watercolor and black chalk on heavily textured paper
28.5 x 21; PT 68

a

b

c

31.

Three Sketches of Tolstoy

ca. 1908; charcoal on paper
(a) 8.2 x 9.7 mm, (b) 14.8 x 8.3 mm,
(c) 21.1 x 16.6 mm
PT (a) 653, (b) 193, (c) 194

32.

Portrait of Mrs. Geduld

1906; oil on canvas
92.8 x 72; PT 350

Mrs. Geduld was the mother of a close family friend who used to play piano duets with Rosalia. This traditional style of portraiture, with its Rembrantesque realism, dark colors, and heavily worked surface is a precursor to Pasternak's experimental, more impressionistic works.

33.

Rachmaninov Playing the Piano

1916; charcoal with traces of red chalk on paper mounted on paper
56 x 45.8; PT 419

Sergei Vasilievich Rachmaninov (1873-1943) was a Russian pianist, composer, and conductor. He was one of the finest pianists of his generation, and also conductor of the Moscow Imperial Opera (1905-6) and of the Philharmonic Concerts (1911-13). He twice refused the conductorship of the Boston Symphony Orchestra. He left Russia in 1917. The painter's son, Alexander Pasternak, in describing his own impressions of the musician, accurately conveys the mood of the portrait: "Rachmaninov was always stern and unsmiling, his movements simple and spare. . . . Every aspect of his personality, as composer, pianist, conductor, and individual of great gentleness and spiritual strength, was expressed in the sobriety and scrupulous simplicity of his performance." (From Ann Pasternak Slater, ed. and trans., *A Vanished Present: The Memoirs of Alexander Pasternak*. London: Harcourt Brace Jovanovich, p. 77.)

34.

Professor Hermann Cohen with Students, Marburg

1912; black chalk on paper mounted on cardboard
29.8 x 26; PT 196

Professor Hermann Cohen (1842-1918) was a distinguished philosopher and founder of the neo-Kantian Marburg School. The Pasternaks had gone to Germany for Rosalia's medical treatment in 1912. Boris spent that summer at the University of Marburg, and can be seen as the tall figure on Professor Cohen's right.

35.

Edward Gordon Craig

1912; black chalk with traces of red chalk on paper
22 x 15; PT 122

Edward Gordon Craig (1872-1966), English designer, producer, and actor, visited Moscow in 1912 to produce Hamlet for the Moscow Arts Theatre, and had a significant effect on Russian stage design in the period before the revolution.

36.

Study of Fedor Chaliapin

1912; black chalk with traces of red chalk on paper
27.5 x 20.3; PT 44

Fedor Ivanovich Chaliapin (1873-1938) was a celebrated Russian operatic bass. In his memoirs, Pasternak recalls, "We used to mark the opening of our yearly Union of Russian Artists exhibitions with . . . a ceremonial dinner at the Hermitage. Apart from the artists who were taking part in the regular exhibition, we also used to invite the artists' friends, art-lovers, collectors, patrons and sometimes performing artists. Chaliapin was nearly always there of course—the artists' best friend. . . . Without ceremony Chaliapin would take his seat at the piano, run his hands over the keys and there would follow a succession of wonderful romances, intimate Russian songs....The music had an intimate quality which you don't get in a concert hall and the fact that it was such an artist as Chaliapin who was singing made it perhaps all the more moving."

37.

Joseph Hoffmann Playing the Piano

1912; black and colored chalks on paper
42.5 x 26.5; PT 101

Joseph Hoffmann (1876-1957) was a child prodigy and then a great pianist. He often performed at the Moscow Conservatory and Philharmonia. (An 1887 article on the phonograph in the *Musical Times* asks, "Will Rubinstein or little Hofmann [sic] make a tour of the world by phonogram, sitting quietly at home. . . ?")

38.

Emil Verhaeren Giving a Poetry Reading

1913; black chalk with traces of red chalk on paper
44 x 30; PT 131

Emil (or Emile) Verhaeren (1855-1916) was a Belgian symbolist poet and critic. He was Flemish, but wrote in French. He is sketched here at a reading he gave in Moscow. This portrait has a touch of caricature, reminiscent of Berlin art of the period.

39.

Einstein Playing the Violin

1927; charcoal on paper
41 x 26; PT 118

Albert Einstein (1879-1955), celebrated physicist, received the Nobel Prize in 1921. At the time of this sketch (1927) he was professor of physics at the Kaiser Wilhelm Institute in Berlin. He was forced from Germany by the Nazis in 1934, and took up a post at the Institute for Advanced Studies, Princeton, which he held until 1945. He became a U.S. citizen in 1940. Pasternak painted Einstein several times (there is an oil portrait at Tel-Aviv University), but the sketches, of which this is a good example, have more life to them. Einstein was a keen amateur violinist, and this energetic drawing captures him in a mood of passionate concentration.

40.

Three Studies of Chaim Weizmann Lecturing

1924; pencil on paper
34 x 26; PT 26

Chaim Weizmann (1874-1952), scientist and Zionist leader, was born in Russia. President of the World Zionist Organization in 1920-31 and in 1935-1946, he was the first President of Israel, 1948-52. This sketch was made during Pasternak's trip to Palestine and Egypt in 1924.

41.

Lenin

ca. 1920; pencil and black chalk on tracing paper
18 x 23; PT 262

This sketch was drawn from life in about 1920. Pasternak was given permission by M. I. Kalinin, the chairman of the All-Union Central Executive Committee (VCIK) and later president of the USSR, to sketch Lenin and other political figures at sessions of the VCIK and at Congresses of the Comintern in the Kremlin. Although only a preliminary outline, this sketch captures Lenin's aggressive intelligence. Another drawing of Lenin by Pasternak hangs in the Kalinin Museum in Moscow.

42.

Lenin

1945; oil on canvas
61 x 46.5; PT 449

Pasternak was working on this portrait during his last year, and it was on his easel when he died, May 31, 1945.

43.

Portrait of the Writer S. Ansky

1918; oil on canvas
68 x 49; PT 446

Shloime Ansky (1863-1920) was a Russian-Jewish author who wrote in Yiddish. He researched regional Jewish folklore, and incorporated elements of it in his stories of peasant life and Hasidism. "Ansky" was a pseudonym; his real name was Rappaport. His best-known work is *The Dybbuk* (published in 1918), a story of demonic possession. Stylistically, Pasternak's portrayal of Ansky stands apart from his other works. The background color and placement of the sitter recall portraits by Ilia Repin, the most prominent figure of nineteenth century realism. Pasternak experimented with Rembrantesque colors and chiaroscuro with a somewhat heavy result; nevertheless, the sitter's character and introspective nature are conveyed.

44.

A Literary Evening at Korzinkino, near Moscow

1918; oil on canvas
41 x 52.3; PT 455

Korzinkino was a village near Moscow. The scene is in the "dacha" (country home) of A. J. Stybel, who appears on the left, beside his second wife. He was a patron of the Jewish arts who commissioned many portraits from Pasternak, thus helping to establish him in his career. Here we see S. Ansky (see cat. 43) reading the manuscript of his story, *The Dybbuk*. The figure with spectacles is David Frischmann, a critic and writer, and the other is a young poet whose name is unknown. The brilliant colors and impressionistic brush work contribute to the animated atmosphere of the painting.

Still Lifes and Scenes of Russia, Palestine, and Germany

Pasternak's informal travel sketches and still lifes are among his most experimental and colorful works. All of these are impressionist in style and show his versatility in approach to new subjects and techniques of sketching in pastel, pencil, and charcoal.

45.

A Vase of Roses

n.d.; oil on canvas
74 x 50.5; PT 614

This still life may have been produced around the time that Pasternak painted *Josephine and Lydia on a Verandah in Molodi*, 1916 (cat. 26).

46.

Woman with Children in a Field

1913; pastel and black chalk on blue Ingres paper
20 x 26.5; PT 260

This field was outside the village of Molodi, near Moscow, where the family spent the summer holidays between 1914 and 1916. Two of the children are the artist's daughters. Pasternak was never without a sketchbook, and being with his wife and children exercised his ability to capture his impressions quickly, which he believed to be essential to portrait painting. He once said that "the nursery is the best exercise for one who wants to master the moving model." This sketch points to Pasternak's admiration for the French *plein-air* painters, especially Bastien-Lepage. (Quoted in David Buckman, *Leonid Pasternak: A Russian Impressionist*. London: Maltzahn Gallery Ltd, 1974, p. 22.)

47.

Horse Pulling a Sledge, Moscow

ca. 1915; pencil, watercolor, gouache, whites, and black chalk on tan paper
31 x 44.5; PT 153

Pasternak has indeed mastered the moving model in this genre scene. The mixed media, layered paint, chalk, and pencil create a complex and very real scene of a horse trudging through mud and snow. Pasternak's realism is neither picturesque nor politically motivated. His interest in "capturing the moment" links him with the Impressionists, and his interest in portraying distinctly "Russian" subjects from the lives of humble people links him with his friend Valentin Serov, who painted many scenes of this sort in the 1890s.

48.

Woman in Traditional Russian Peasant Costume

ca. 1905; charcoal and watercolor on heavy paper
21.2 x 13.6; PT 159

In the same spirit as *A Horse Pulling a Sledge* (cat. 47), this work emerges out of Russian realist traditions. Realist painters like Sergi Vasilievich Ivanov also explored themes about Russian village life; the difference here is that this work is a straightforward study with no didactic purpose.

49.

Night View, Moscow

ca. 1915; watercolor, gouache, pastel, and pencil on dark, blue-green paper
21.4 x 27; PT 54

This and *Winter View, Moscow* (cat. 50) were taken from the artist's apartment on the Volkhonka, a medieval street near what is today the Pushkin Museum. The view was of the square around the Cathedral of Christ the Savior and the pink-and-white bell tower of the Blessed Virgin, with its dome and cross. Along with *View of the Kremlin* (cat. 51), these impressionistic cityscapes make an evocative series of pre-revolutionary Moscow scenes.

50.

Winter View, Moscow

1917; watercolor and gouache on beige cardboard
32 x 24.2; PT 66

51.

Winter View of the Kremlin

1917; gouache, watercolor, and pencil on tan paper
34.4 x 24.3; PT 62

Landmarks such as the sixteenth century bell tower of Ivan the Great and the Domes of the Kremlin churches are integrated with a more prosaic foreground scene.

52.

Road Scene by the Tomb of Rachel, Palestine

1924; charcoal on tracing paper
29 x 38.4; PT 87

Pasternak was offered the opportunity to join a group of artists for a short visit to Palestine in 1924. The colors and exotic landscape captivated him, and he made a very large number of rapid sketches in the course of a hectic tour.

53.

Two Palestine Scenes

1924; pastel on paper; pastel and watercolor on paper

14.8 x 20.8, 10.5 x 15.5; PT 487, 525

a

b

54.

Arab Woman Milking a Goat

1924; watercolor and black chalk
on grey wove paper
32 x 24.4; PT 7

56.

Schoolboys in Palestine

1924: charcoal on paper 25 x 16.5; PT 415

55.

Head of an Old Man, Palestine

1924; charcoal and chalk on paper
35.6 x 28; PT 130

57.

Village of Feldafing on the Starnbergersee, near Munich

1932-33; watercolor on paper
21 x 28.8; PT 77

The artist moved to Germany with his wife and daughters in 1921, to seek medical help for his wife unavailable at that time in the USSR. The two sons visited them there in 1923, but returned to Moscow. Leonid and his wife had long-term plans to return to Russia, but Rosalia's death and the onset of the war meant that these were never fulfilled. During this period in Germany, from 1921 to 1938, Leonid and Rosalia spent most summers in Bavaria, where his two daughters lived. This charming, impressionist-style landscape is from their holidays in 1932-33. Larissa Salmina-Haskell has noted that similar studies appear in the painter's sketchbook dated 1932. The vivid colors in the painting are characteristic of Pasternak's German period.

58.

Berlin Street Scene

n.d.; watercolor on paper
23.7 x 16; PT 125

The view is from the window of the artist's apartment on Bayreutherstrasse in Berlin, where the Pasternaks lived in 1923-24. The gasometer, depicted in bright orange, lends the picture an air of modernism.

59.

Watermelon

n.d.; watercolor on paper
18 x 25; PT 124

Stylistically these vivid still lifes belong to Pasternak's Berlin period. The forms are created from layers and layers of thin but richly colored watercolors.

60.

Still Life with Black Grapes

1932; watercolor on paper
21 x 28.5; PT 110

Selected Bibliography

Buckman, David. *Leonid Pasternak: A Russian Impressionist.* London: Maltzahn Gallery Ltd, 1974.

Crawford Centre for the Arts, University of St. Andrews. *Exhibition of Works by Leonid Pasternak: 1862-1945.* Introduction by Larissa Salmina-Haskell, essay by Jennifer Bradshaw. St. Andrews, Scotland, 1978.

Gomberg-Verzhbinskaya, E.P. *Peredvizhnik.* Leningrad: Iskusstvo, 1970.

Hilton, Alison. "Scenes from Life and Contemporary History." In *Russian Realism of the 1870s-1880s in the European Realist Tradition,* edited by Gabriel P. Weisberg. Bloomington: Indiana University Press, 1982.

Lapshin, V.P. *Soiuz Russkikh Khudozhnikov.* Leningrad: Khudozhnik RSFSR, 1974.

Loukomski, George K. *History of Modern Russian Painting (Russian Painting of the Past Hundred Years, 1840-1940).* London: Hutchinson & Co., 1945.

Osborn, Max. *Leonid Pasternak.* Warsaw: Stybel, 1932.

Pasternak, Boris. *I Remember: Sketch for an Autobiography.* Translated by David Magarshak. New York: Meridian, 1960.

Pasternak, Leonid. *The Memoirs of Leonid Pasternak.* Translated by Jennifer Bradshaw, introduction by Josephine Pasternak. London: Quartet Books, 1982.

Pasternak, Leonid. *Zapisi raznykh let.* Moscow: Sovetskii Khudozhnik, 1975.

Pasternak Slater, Ann, ed. and trans. *A Vanished Present: The Memoirs of Alexander Pasternak.* London: Harcourt Brace Jovanovich, 1984.

Rice, Tamara Talbot. *A Concise History of Russian Art.* New York: Frederick A. Praeger, 1963.

Russell, John. "Pasternak." *Studio* 161, no. 815 (March 1961).

Russia, The Land, The People: Russian Painting, 1850-1910. Washington D.C.: Smithsonian Institution Traveling Exhibition Service/Seattle: University of Washington Press, 1986.

Sakharova, E., ed. *V.D. Polenov—E.D. Plenova. Khroniki sem'i khudozhnikov.* Moscow: Iskusstvo, 1964.

Sarabianov, Dmitrii Vladimirovich. *Russian Painters of the Early Twentieth Century (New Trends).* In English and Russian. Leningrad: Aurora Art Publishers, 1973.

Sternin, Grigori. *Khudozhestvennaia Zhivn' Rossii Na Rubezhe XIX-XX Vekov* (*Artistic Life of Russia at the Turn of the 19th-20th Century*). In Russian. Moscow: Iskusstvo, 1970.

Valkenier, Elizabeth. *Russian Realist Art. The State and Society: The Peredvizhniki and Their Tradition.* Ann Arbor: Ardis, 1977.

Prepared by the Smithsonian Institution Traveling Exhibition Service
Andrea Price Stevens, Publications Director
Edited by David Andrews, SITES
Designed by Gerard A. Valerio, Bookmark Studio, Annapolis, Maryland
Composed in Bembo by Composition Systems Inc.,
Falls Church, Virginia
Printed on Mohawk Superfine by Collins Lithographic, Inc.,
Baltimore, Maryland